Fighting Colors

F4U-CORSAIR in Color

by Jim Sullivan

illustrated by Don Greer

squadron/signal publications

ISBN 0-89747-120-2

If you have any photographs of the aircraft, armor, soldiers or ships of any nation, particularly wartime snapshots, why not share them with us and help make Squadron/Signal's books all the more interesting and complete in the future. Any photograph sent to us will be copied and the original returned. The donor will be fully credited for any photos used. Please send them to: Squadron/Signal Publications, Inc., 1115 Crowley Dr., Carrollton, TX 75006.

Dedication

This book is dedicated to the thousands of Navy and Marine pilots who flew the Corsair in war and peace and to the memory of those who made the ultimate sacrifice that we might enjoy liberty and freedom.

List of Contributors

The author wishes to thank the following people for their assistance in providing photographic and research material: Hal Andrews, Cdr. R.E. Bennett, USN Ret., Peter Bowers, Bob Cressman, Michael Cristesco, Ronald Gerdes, Clay Jansson, Bill Larkins, Bob Lawson, Paul McDaniel, Walt Ohlrich, Art Schoeni, Paul Stevens and Bob Stuckey. Special thanks are noted to M/Sgt. Fritz Gemeinhardt, USMC Ret., and Richard Hill for their continued support in providing detailed information and photographic material. Also the Vought Corporation, The National Archives and the USMC History Center.

F4U-1 No. 18 carries the Jolly Roger flag of VF-17 on the side of the engine cowling. This three-toned Corsair is flying from *USS Bunker Hill* during their shakedown cruise, July 1943. It is in standard three-color camouflage, non-specular Sea Blue, intermediate Blue and White. (National Archives)

Glossy Sea Blue F4U-1Ds and FG-1Ds of VF-84, VMF-221 and VMF-451 turn-up prior to launching from *Bunker Hill*. In a matter of minutes, these Yellow nosed aircraft will be headed toward Iwo Jima to give ground support to the Marine invasion there, February 1945. (National Archives)

To increase the range of the F4U, the 237-gallon internal fuel tank was supplemented by a 160-gallon drop tank. The 2000hp P&W R-2800-8W engine consumed 195 gallons of fuel per hour during normal rated cruise. Vought Plant, 16 June 1943. Note that this early machine is still in the two-tone Blue Grey/Light Grey scheme with the early Blue roundel insignia. (Chance Vought)

Corsair in Color

The specifications for the XF4U-1 Corsair as outlined on April 26, 1940 by Vought-Sikorsky Aircraft required a single engine, single seat landplane fighter that could be used aboard aircraft carriers. Specifically, it should be able to take-off from the deck of an aircraft carrier with or without the aid of a catapult and land on the carrier deck with arresting gear or land on an ordinary landing field.

The XF4U-1 was powered by a Pratt and Whitney R-2800-4 two-stage engine rated at 1,850hp for take-off. In a 15 knot wind it could get airborne in 338 feet and climb to 15,000 feet in 5.8 minutes.

The XF4U-1 was the subject of an early 40's newspaper article which called it a "Super Stuka" stating that "...tactically it is a flying destroyer, able to dive right through a hail of machine gun bullets and sink an enemy cruiser with either a torpedo or bombs." More exact details of the testing of the Corsair followed quoting from the actual experiences of a Navy test pilot, James B. Taylor, Jr. who was challenged to show the effects of pull out from a 10-G dive..."Taylor calmly climbed to 20,000 feet...when he reached diving altitude...he checked the time...closing the throttle he rolled the ship over on its back and headed for the target on the ground...Taylor recognized the familiar stiffness paralyzing the controls as the speed passed 500mph...the altimeter unwound backward like the hand of a clock whose works had gone haywire. Suddenly he began to see details on the ground...he took another look at his instruments and yanked back on the stick." As pull out occurred, Taylor..."began to experience...discomfort, flesh sagged from his face, eyeballs bulged, breath sighed from his lungs...the Corsair changed directions, then rocketed skyward on its own momentum...Taylor then spiraled down for a perfect landing...when the engineers removed the accelerometer they were incredulous to discover a reading of 13-Gs." the 165 lb. pilot at the moment of pull out had withstood a force of about 2,000 lbs.

The first production F4U-1 (02153) was flown on June 25, 1942 in the standard Navy colors of non-specular blue-grey on the top areas of the Corsair and the undersides of the outer wing panels with non-specular light grey on the bottom surfaces. Six position roundels were applied with a white star on a dark blue field. The prop blades were non-specular black with four inch bands of orange-yellow and red at the tip. Very little stenciling appeared on any of the F4Us and the early versions often carried only the one inch black lettering on the fin and rudder that identified the aircraft type, the assigned Bureau Number and the branch of service (Navy or Marine). From this first F4U delivered in 1942, 12,581 more would follow until January of 1953 when the production line was shut down. Final figures show the following production breakdown:

F4U-1 No. 57 of VMF-216 is seen on the strip just recently liberated from the Japanese at Torokina Point, Bougainville, 10 December 1943. The 57 in white is the aircraft number assigned by the Squadron Commander. (USMC)

Vought

XF4U-1	1
F4U-1 (Includes F4U-1A)	2814
F4U-1C	200
F4U-1D	1685
F4U-4 (All versions)	2357
F4U-5 (All versions)	568
AU-1	111
F4U-7	94

Goodyear

FG-1 (Includes FG-1A)	2010
FG-1D	1997
F2G	10

Brewster

F3A-1 (Includes F3A-1A)	735

Major William Gise of VMF-124 is credited with taking the first Marine Corsairs into combat during February of 1943. Nine months later, VF-17 led by Cdr. Tom Blackburn brought the first Corsair-equipped Navy squadron into combat with the Japanese during late October, 1943.

1st Lt. Ken Walsh seen in plane No. 13 of VMF-124 (Walsh ended the war with 21 victories). The plane crew prepares to kick the wheel chocks and assist during taxi. Note the white painted outlines on the wing gun openings, the outboard fourth 'gun' is painted on for effect. The word CAPTAIN appears on the starboard dive brake fairing, Russell Islands, 1 September 1943. (USMC)

One of the first Corsairs to come aboard the Enterprise was F4U-1 No. 82, flown by Swede Vejtasa during a training cruise, in the standard Blue-Grey/Light Grey scheme with White numbers. The aircraft number is repeated on the wing panels and this machine sports the six postion roundels, 20 March 1943. (National Archives)

F4U-1, 17590 of VMF-223 during an engine change on Vella Lavella, 10 December 1943. The 590 split stenciled in white is taken from the last three digits of the aircraft Bureau Number (BuNo). The national insignia has been updated by having White bars added to the Blue roundel. (National Archives)

The production F4U-1 had a combat gross weight of 12,061 lbs. and was powered by a R-2800-8 two-stage engine which allowed the Corsair to reach a speed of 415mph under war-emergency power. In a 25 knot wind, the F4U-1 could be airborne under normal take-off power in 340 feet and could reach a service ceiling of 37,200 feet. The F4U-1 was modified early in the production run to an improved style canopy with better visibility than the original "greenhouse" version. This modification is often referred to as the F4U-1A/FG-1A although officially the Corsair was listed as the F4U-1/FG-1 until the "C" and "D" versions were produced.

In February of 1943 the USN issued directives that changed the two color Blue-Grey/Light Grey scheme to a three tone scheme changing all upper surfaces to a semi-gloss Sea Blue, the fuselage sides and undersides of the outer wing panels to non-specular intermediate Blue and the bottom areas to a non-specular insignia White. In addition to this, the National insignia was changed to a four position arrangement with Red-outlined White bars added to the roundel. Prop blades remained Black but were changed to have only one four inch Orange-Yellow band at the tip. Wheel wells for the main gear and tailwheel assembly were Green-tinted zinc chromate while wheel well doors inside and out were non-specular insignia White. The instrument panel and forward areas of the cockpit including the insides of the windscreen framing were semi-gloss instrument Black, while the remainder of the cockpit interior was zinc chromate tinted with interior Green. In September of 1943 the Red surround on the National insignia was replaced with an insignia Blue outline on all four positions.

During WWII, the F4U was regarded by many pilots to be the best Naval or Marine fighter flying. Pilots and groundcrew developed and mastered the technique of dive bombing with the fighter and indeed established the fighter-bomber concept. Rigged with a centerline rack at first, F4U-1As roared off South Pacific islands with 500 lb. bombs bringing destruction to the Japanese island strongholds.

The F4U-1D/FG-1D was the next version that expanded the capabilities of the Corsair. Provisions were made to carry a pair of bombs or napalm or fuel tanks on wing root pylons as well the addition of rocket launching stubs for eight air-to-ground rockets. Some of the other WWII modifications to the Corsair included the addition of a camera installation for photo-reconnaissance work and the installation of radar equipment in 24 aircraft to allow night fighting capability. Some of the lesser known modifications included one example of a two-seat trainer; another was used as a flying testbed for a Westinghouse jet engine and several others were used in JATO (Jet Assisted Take-Off) tests. Perhaps the most potentially successful modification was achieved when F4U-1 02460 was modified to take the 3,000hp Wasp Major engine. This "Super-Corsair" was to evolve into the bubble canopy F2G series. The Navy initially ordered 418 of these aircraft but only ten were actually built before the remainder of the contract was cancelled as WWII drew to a close.

In March of 1944 the Navy once again issued directives to change the color scheme of Naval and Marine aircraft. The three tone scheme was replaced by an overall finish of glossy Sea Blue which was to remain with the Corsair line through WWII and the Korean War. The F4U in the glossy Sea Blue finish retained the same cockpit colors as before and its Blue-outlined National insignia until the late 40's when the borderless style insignia was slowly cycled into general use as the Corsair went through O&R. In 1947, a Red stripe was added to the White bars in the National insignia.

Meanwhile, Vought, continuing to improve the Corsair line, produced the F4U-4 version with a more powerful R-2800-18W engine that under combat conditions and at 20,000 feet could make 440mph. With a lower stall speed of 73 knots, the F4U-4 delivered overall improved performance in all areas. Especially welcomed by the pilots was the improved cockpit arrangement that made this Corsair easier to handle than the F4U-1 series. F4U-4 service ceiling under military power settings was 41,200 feet. Delivered just in time to see WWII combat, the first F4U-4s saw action with the USMC on Okinawa in June of 1945.

The war in the Pacific was over in August of 1945 and the Corsair was to see five years of peace before once again being called on in 1950 to fight in the Korean war. During this five year interlude Vought had produced yet another version of the bent-wing fighter, the F4U-5. Faster than any of the production Corsairs thusfar, the F4U-5 was powered by a R-2800-32 two-stage engine — at 20,000 feet the aircraft could reach 466mph and had a service ceiling of 41,400 feet. Most of the previous Corsairs had been armed with six 50 cal. machine guns (exceptions being the F4U-1C and F4U-4B) but Vought produced the F4U-5 with four 20mm cannons that carried a total of 924 rounds.

The USN and USMC used the F4U-4 and F4U-5 variants during the first year and a half of the Korean War and in mid-1952, AU-1s, the final U.S. version joined the fight. In July of 1953 a truce was signed in Korea and hostilities ceased. This was the last time Corsairs of the USN and USMC saw combat. By the end of the 1950s Corsairs were replaced by newer, faster jet aircraft.

During WWII Corsairs were provided to and flown by England and New Zealand...after Korea additional Corsairs were to see action with the military forces of France (a specially produced version, the F4U-7) and with Honduras, El Salvador and Argentina.

In late 1956, the Navy issued orders that dramatically changed the appearance of Naval and Marine aircraft. The glossy Sea Blue was out; the new colors were to be Gull Grey tops and Insignia White bottoms, ailerons, flaps and elevators. Four-position Blue-outlined National insignias were back on the aircraft. This final scheme came along at a time when very few Corsairs were still flying and as a result only a handful of examples were ever so painted. These were AES-12 AU-1s from MCAS Quantico and a half-dozen or so reserve F4U-4s.

The accomplishments of the Corsair line for the most part are a matter of record and have been retold numerous times. The 1950-51 cruise book of the USS Essex comes close to summing up the feelings of those who knew the Corsair..."compared to the speed of a jet, the Hose Nose was slow. And it was common gossip that the Fox-4-Uncles were one of the largest users of sealing wax, baling wire and band-aids. But when it came to delivering the goods, the Corsair took a back seat to no plane. Hustling down the deck, the F4U knew the way to and from battle better than any other plane on board. Since early in World War II, the Corsair had built up a reputation for a job well-done. There had been a modification here, and an improvement there since the first model had come off the line. But, by and large this was the same plane that had roared through the skies over Guadalcanal, the Marshalls, over Iwo and Guam, up and down Samar and Honshu and Okinawa. True, faster planes were out. Planes were aboard that could carry heavier loads. But, when it came to delivering the goods, the Corsair took a back seat to no plane. The men who flew the Hose Nose had a reason to be proud."

Today, over 40 years after the first flight of the XF4U-1, a handful of Corsairs are still airworthy. After expensive restoration most of these aircraft fly at airshows so we may be thrilled to the exhilarating sound of a powerful past-guardian of the skies as it whistles overhead...a graceful, beautiful bird.

Maj. Gregory 'Pappy' Boyington, CO of VMF-214, in the cockpit of F4U-1A, 17883, ready to taxi from its revetment on Vella Lavella. Note the red surround on the fuselage insignia, November 1943. (National Archives)

F4U-1A, 17875, of VMF-212 in a three-tone finish, skidded off Torokina Field during take-off. The pilot was uninjured and the Corsair needed only a new prop, 20 December 1943. (USMC)

F4U-1As of VMF-217 taxi out for an escort mission, shepherding bombers headed for Rabaul. Bougainville, 10 February 1944. (USMC)

(Above) F4U-1A, 17884 of VMF-214 and 17840 of VMF-222 have ended their war contribution, and with many parts 'canabalized', rot in a jungle boneyard on Bougainville, January 1944. (National Archives)

(Left) F4U-1A No. 36 landing long on board *Bunker Hill*. VF-17 Corsairs were heading toward the South Pacific and combat, 14 September 1943. Note the Red surround to the national insignia. (National Archives)

(Right) F4U-1A, 56240, of VMF-223 flying escort for a Navy PBY standing by to pick up pilots who have gone down in the sea. The Catalina was based in the Stirling Islands, 3 May 1944. (USMC)

(Below) A white-nosed FG-1A, 14220, from VMF-114 is loaded with napalm (in the early-style drop tanks) for strikes against Japanese dug in on Bloody Nose Ridge on Peleliu, October 1944. (USMC)

(Right) Yellow-nosed glossy Sea Blue F4U-1Ds and FG-1Ds of VF-84 prepare to launch from *Bunker Hill* for an attack on Iwo Jima. Note the use of the white sealing tape just forward of the cockpit, 19 February 1945. (National Archives)

(Below Right) Cannon-armed glossy Sea Blue F4U-1Cs of VMF-311 taxi for take-off from Yontan airfield on Okinawa to begin a Combat Air Patrol mission, drop tanks are insignia White. 26 April 1945. (USMC)

(Below Left) With her name in Yellow, *Jeanne*, a F4U-1C of VMF-311 is mired in the Okinawa mud. The four 20mm cannons had a total of 880 rounds of ammunition, April 1945. (USMC)

(Bottom) F4U-1D, 82526, of VBF-99 carries the White fuselage marking, L19. The one-wheel landing was made when the right landing gear failed to extend, NAB Marpi, Saipan. The wing tip stripe in White is repeated on the lower left wing tip. 31 May 1945. (National Archives)

This glossy Sea Blue F4U-1D No. 97 of VMF-913 is piloted by Lt. Marvin out of MCAS Cherry Point, NC. The F4U-1D featured the option of carrying rockets, bombs and/or drop tank. The marking F-97 is in White. Between Vought and Goodyear, 3,682 'D' models were built. (Bob Hall)

FG-1D 88038 launches from the *Sargent Bay*. This Corsair was soon assigned to VMF-512 and participated in strikes against Okinawa. 2 June 1945. (National Archives)

2nd Lt. Marvin Bristow and his mechanic stand in front of fully loaded F4U-1D No. 207. VMF-224 was the only fighter unit to carry the individual White aircraft number in this position, just aft of the cowl flaps. Note the three kill marks below the canopy, Okinawa, 5 May 1945. (USMC)

F4U-1

F4U-1, 02576, of VMF-222 stationed at Torokina Field on Bougainville. The 'Flying Deuces' participated in the first fighter sweeps on Rabaul, December 1943.

F4U-1 Details

Gun Switch Box

F4U-1 Cockpit

Rocket Station Distributor Box Installed on F4U-1/FG-1Ds

Mk 8 Gunsight

F4U-1 Seat, Armoured Head Rest & Oxygen Bottle

F4U-1 Details

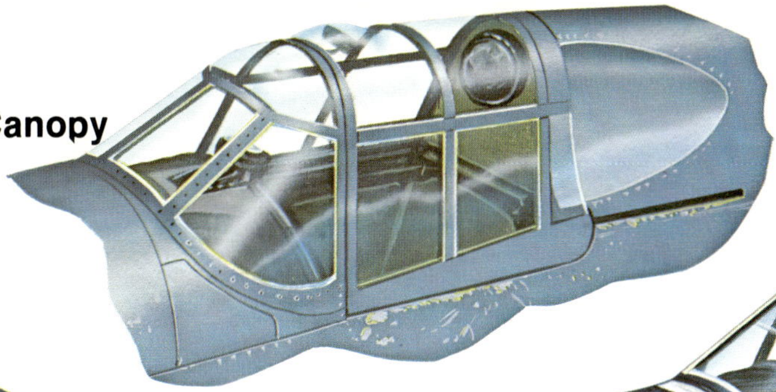

F4U-1 Canopy

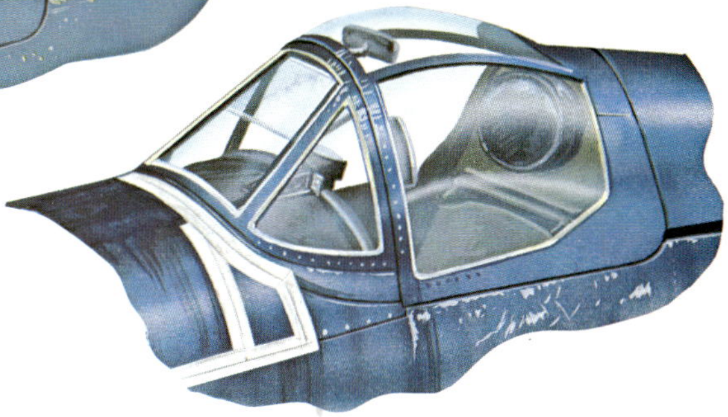

F4U-1A Canopy

F4U-1 Wing with Fabric Outer Wing Panels

Control Stick

Marine Pilot, 1943

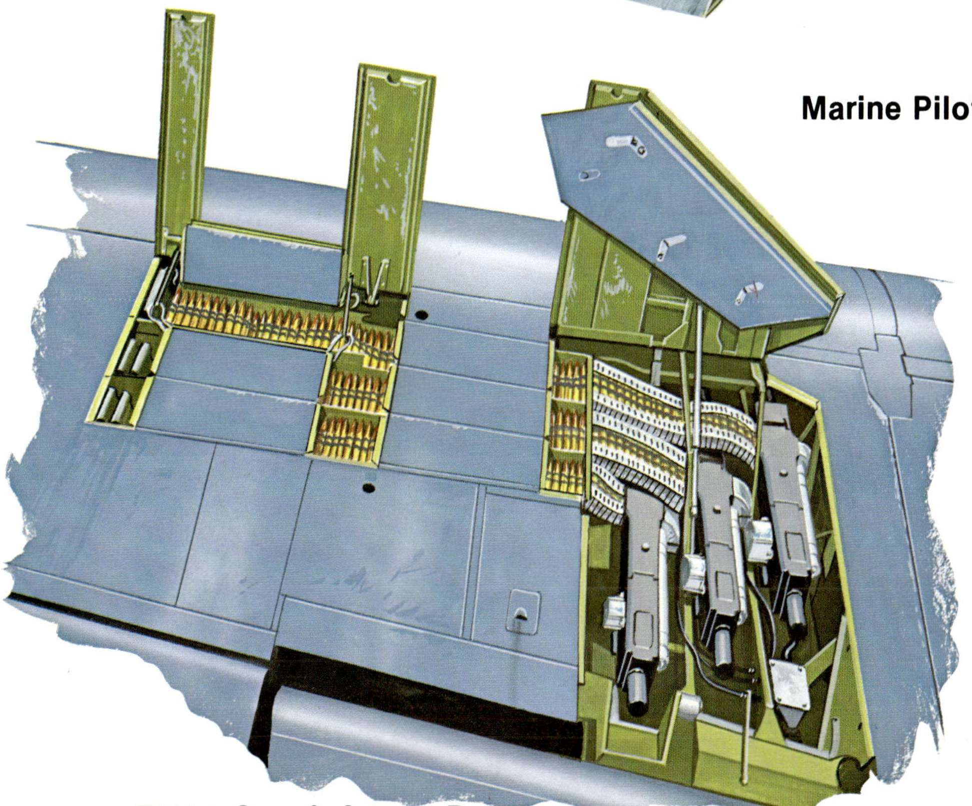

F4U-1 Gun & Ammo Bays

F4U-1 Details

Inner Wing Section Showing Main Gear Wells

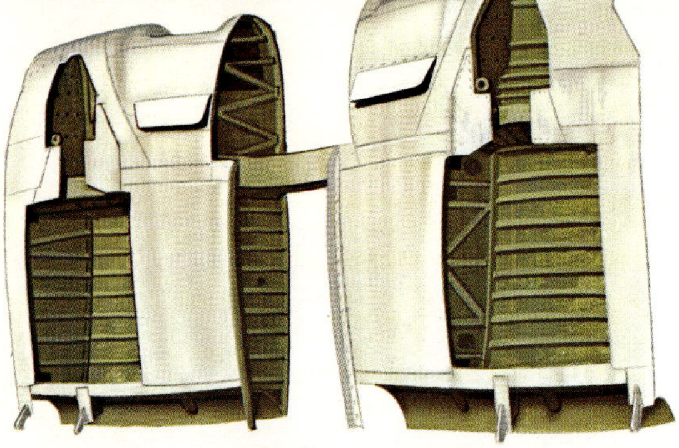

Tailwheel & Arresting Hook

Main Landing Gear

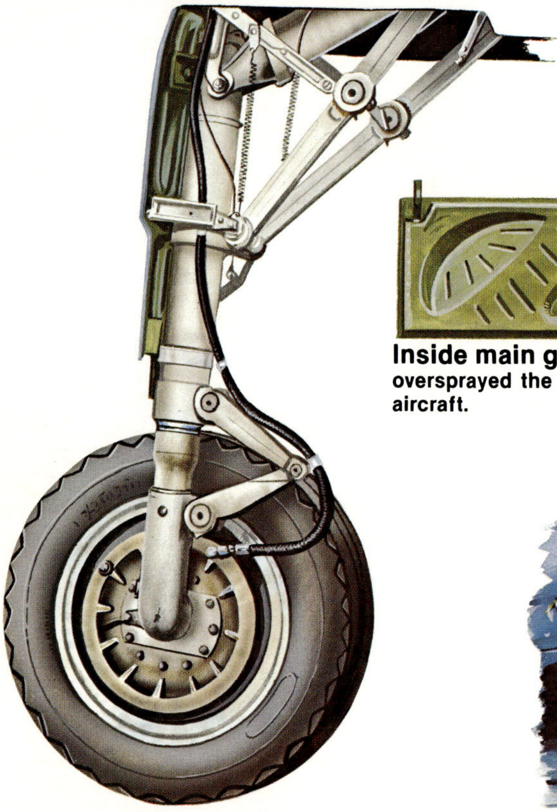

Inside main gear doors. These were sometimes oversprayed the same color as the underside of the aircraft.

Oil Cooler & Intercooler Intake

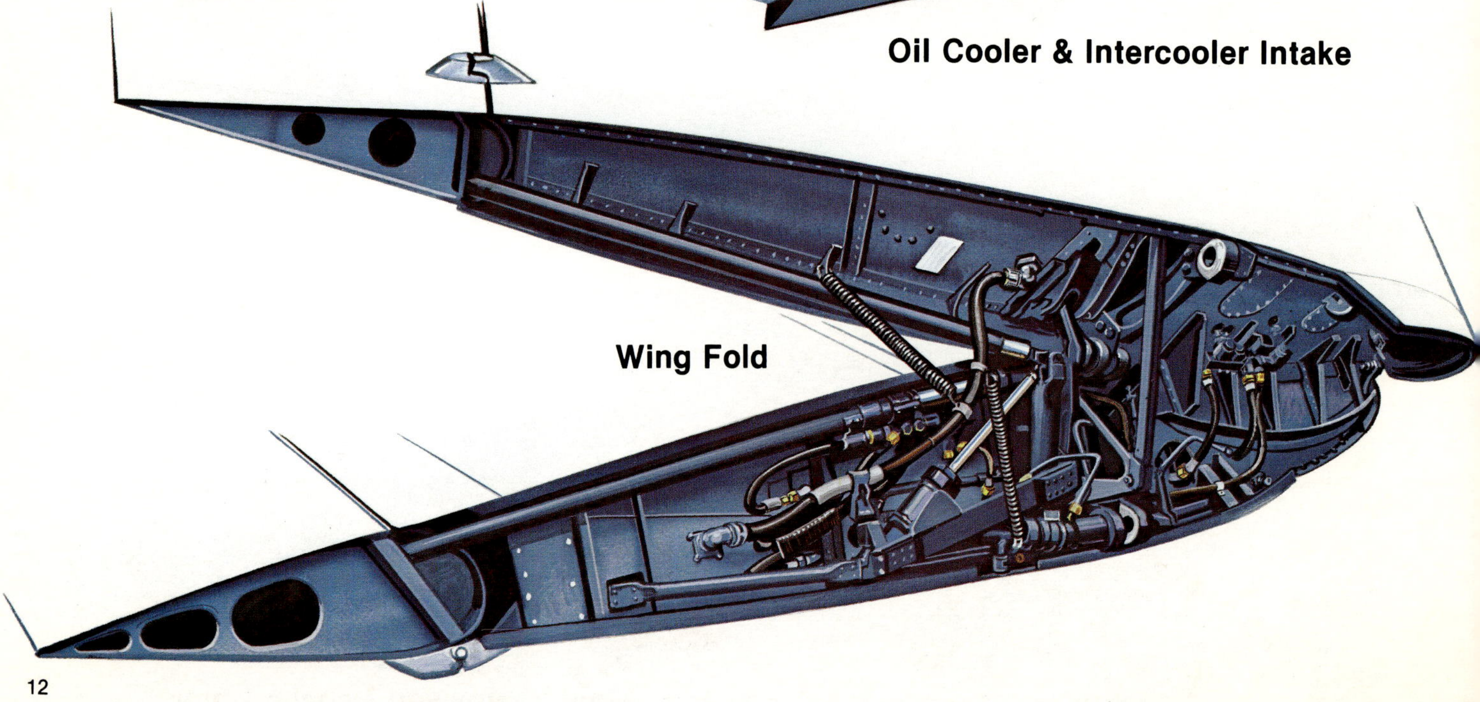

Wing Fold

F4U-1 Details

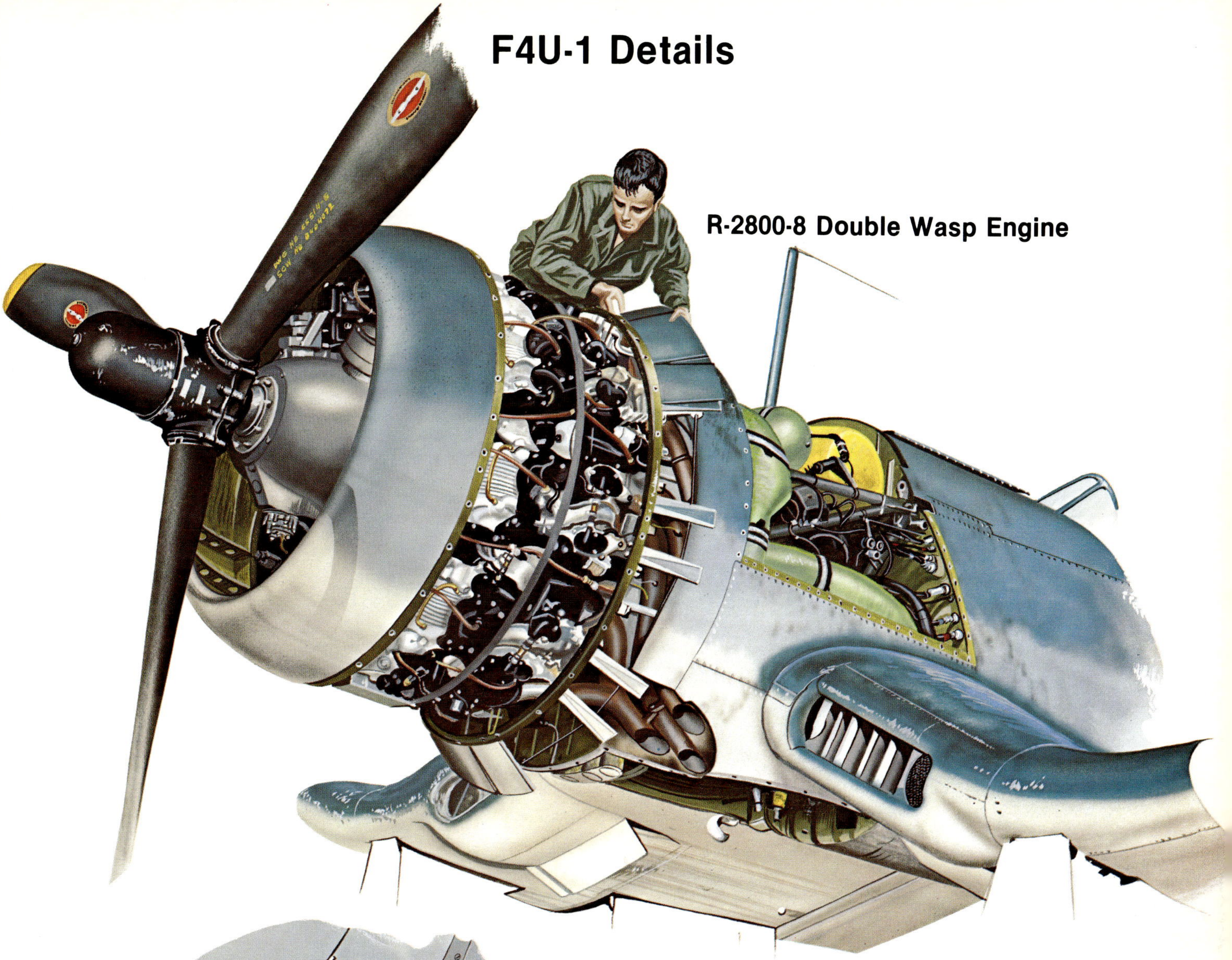

R-2800-8 Double Wasp Engine

1000 lb. HE Bomb on Brewster Bomb Rack

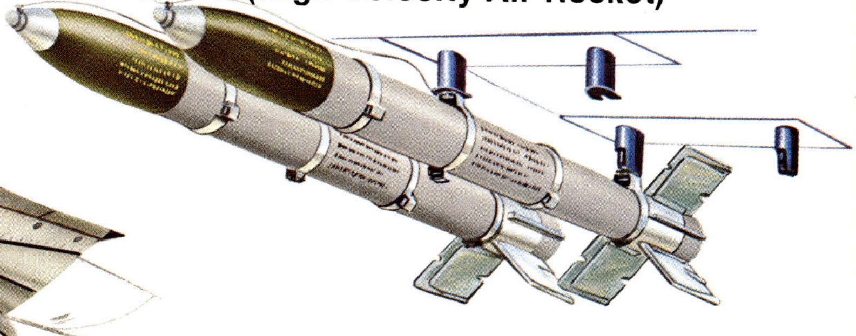

5" HVAR (High Velocity Air Rocket)

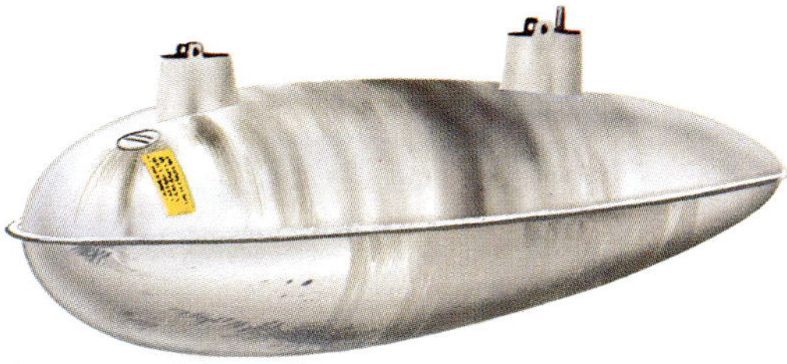

Center Line Drop-Tank (175 Gal.)

Bomb Trolley

Field-Improvised Napalm Bomb

F4U-1

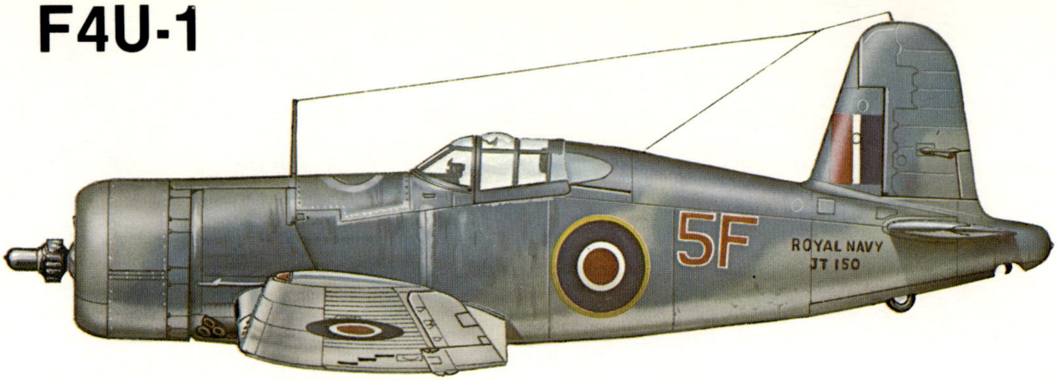

F4U-1, 18172, JT150, of The Royal Navy 1835 Sqn., at NAS Brunswick, Maine, October 1943.

VF-17 Emblem

F4U-1, 02337, of VF-17 from the *USS Bunker Hill*, July 1943. This Corsair was flown by Jim Halford who had four previous kills in F4Fs at Guadalcanal.

F4U-1A, 17777, of VMF-214, "Blacksheep" Squadron, Torokina Field, Bougainville, December 1943.

FG-1A, 14056, of VMF-122, "Mary" flown by Maj. "Effie" Pierce, Peleliu, November 1944. The Corsair was named for Maj. Pierce's wife.

FG-1A, 14208, of VMF-114, from Peleliu, October 1944 participated in U.S. Marine Napalm attacks on Bloody Nose Ridge.

FG-1A, 14525, of VMF-313, based at Leyte, Philippine Islands, December 1944.

F4U-1D of VBF-6, stationed aboard the USS Hancock, **March, 1945.**

FG-1D, No.99 of HQSS-22 (Headquarters Service Sqn.) on Ie Shima, Ryukyu Islands, June 1945.

F4U-1D, No.82 of VMF-511, "Daisy June", on the USS Block Island, **July 1945.**

FG-1A, 14776, KD345 of 1850 Sqn. on board the HMS Vengeance, **December 1945.**

F4U-4

F4U-4, 81993, No.059 of VMF-225, one of the aircraft selected to represent the USMC during the National Air Races in Cleveland, Ohio, September 1946.

F4U-4 Details

F4U-4 Cockpit

F4U-4 Pilot

Control Stick & Grip

F4U-4 Seat & Armoured Headrest

F4U-4 Details

F4U-4 Cowling

F4U-4B Underwing Rocket Rails & Anti-Tank Rocket

Standard 150 gal. Drop Tank

Underwing Pylon with 1000 lb. Bomb

F4U-4 Showing Wing Step in Flap, Flap Slitter Plate and Cowl Flap/Exhaust

F4U-4

F4U-4, 81924 of VMF-211 China, 1945. One of the few F4U-4s to become operational during WWII.

F4U-4, 80887, of VF-22, stationed on board the USS Coral Sea, 1948.

F4U-4, 80846 of VF-14 stationed at NAS Jacksonville, Florida, September 1949.

F4U-4B, 62969 No.16 of VMA-332 from the USS Bairoko, off Korea, July 1953.

F4U-4, 97264, No.11 from the Naval Air Reserve Training Unit, based at NAS Olathe, Kansas, March 1956.

F4U-5N

F4U-5N, 123191, No.16 of VMF(N)-513, the "Flying Nightmares, operating from Wonsan, Korea, November 1950.

F4U-5 Details

F4U-5N Cockpit

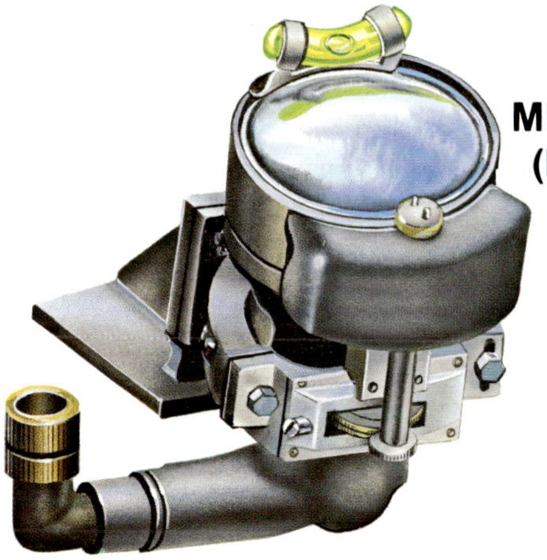

Mk 8 Gunsight (F4U-5 & 5P)

Mk 20 Gunsight (F4U-5N)

USN/USMC Pilots, Korea 1952

F4U-5 Details

Ground crew using pressurized refueling equipment on F4U-5N.

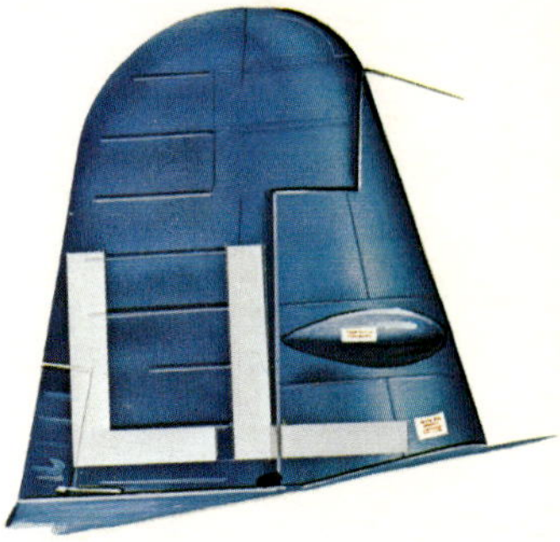

F4U-5P Bulged Fin (for compass transmitter)

F4U-5P Camera Port

F4U-5NL Retractable Step

20MM Gun Flash Hiders & Gun Camera Shield

De-Icer Boot

AN/APS-19A Radar

F4U-5

F4U-5, 122066 No.14 of VMA-324 stationed at NAS Miami, Florida, November 1952.

F4U-5P, 122169 No.24 of VC-62 served aboard the *USS Boxer* off Korea, September 1950.

F4U-5N, 124449 No.11 of VMF(N)-513, in one-of-a-kind flat Black paint scheme. Kunsan, Korea (K-8) 1952.

F4U-5P, 121977, of VC-61, on board the *USS Valley Forge* off Korea, July 1950.

F4U-5N, 124713 of VC-3 seen at airshow at Milwaukee, Wisconsin, 1954.

AU-1, 129401, No.24 of VMA-323 at Chin Chan, Korea (K-47), Summer 1952.

AU-1, 129378 of SOES-12, flown by Col. John Bolt, MCAS El Toro, California, 1957.

F4U-5NL, 124541, stationed aboard The Independencia, of the Argentine Navy, 1962.

AU-1, 129378, No. 15 of Flottille 17F, Telergma, Algeria, 1961. This is the same aircraft flown earlier by Col. John Bolt.

F4U-7, 133657, of Flottille 14F at Cuers Naval Air Base, France, March 1964.

New to the combat area, the Vought-built F4U-4 Corsair provided all-around improved performance over the F4U-1. Seen above are the dash 4s of VMF-223 just arrived at Okinawa, June 1945. Overall glossy Sea Blue, the White fuselage numbers are the last three digits of the aircraft Bureau Number. (USMC)

F4U-4 No. 99 of VBF-89 taxis on board *Antietam* during its shakedown cruise. The P&W R-2800-18W engine turned a 13' 1" Hamilton Standard four-bladed prop. Note the taped-over gun ports to reduce drag. All lettering is White. 14 March 1945. (National Archives)

White trim on the prop hub, fin tip and tail cone were the markings VMF-212 applied to its Corsairs. F4U-4 No. 6 is BuNo. 80874 and is taxiing to the runway for a strike against the Japanese home islands. Okinawa, June 1945. (USMC)

F4U-4, 81150, No. 109 in the post-war markings of Air Training Unit VF-1 flies over the Florida countryside near NAS Jacksonville. The numbers are White but the letters 'CA' are in Yellow and the strip just behind the cowl flaps, normally in glossy Sea Blue, is unpainted burnished aluminum. October 1947. (National Archives)

F4U-4, 81246, of VBF-17 shows off the rocket rail installation and wing fold detail. The cowl insignia is a skeleton in cowboy garb riding an alligator while delivering a bomb and bullets. The fuselage lettering in White is '17BF62', c.1946. (via Robert O'Dell)

F4U-4 No. 1 of VF-61 carries fuselage marking No. 101 in White just forward of the borderless national insignia. The No. 2 Corsair retains the bordered style, while 101 and 104 do not. All aircraft display the Jolly Roger emblem. 1949. (via Rex B. Beisel)

(Above) 'WE 14', a glossy Sea Blue F4U-4B of VMF-214 carries birthday greetings in celebration of the 176th anniversary of the United States Marine Corps. These greetings in the form of two napalm bombs from the Blacksheep squadron were delivered to North Korea. The F4U-4B differed from the F4U-4 in cannon armament and the position of the rocket launcher stubs, 10 November 1951. (USMC)

F4U-4, 96887, of VX-3 carries a standard Navy 150-gallon drop tank. Note the pattern of the split stenciling in White on the fuselage and rudder, also the heavily worn paint just forward of the cockpit and on the wing. This Corsair has the later-style blown canopy, c.1952. (Walt Ohlrich)

F4U-4, 97075, of VF-742 warms up prior to departure after its stopover at Wilmington, NC. The footstep shows up against the inboard section of the flaps which are set at the full deflection of 50 degrees. All markings including the tip of the rudder are White. 1951. (Paul McDaniel)

A loose gas cap on its drop tank was the cause of this fire as F4U-4, 96821, was recovering on board *Sicily* off Korea. This machine, No. 13, belongs to VMF-323 Deathrattlers. 11 June 1951. (USMC)

F4U-4, 80960, No. 16 of VBF-4 slid to a grinding halt at NAS Chincoteague, VA. This bellied-in Corsair has its tailwheel extended while the front of the aircraft seems to be resting on its dive brake fairings and landing gear doors. Rudder markings in Yellow, all others are White. 26 January 1946. (National Archives)

Rocket and napalm armed F4U-4 of VF-884 warms up for take off from the *USS Boxer* off the Korean coast. 19 May 1951. (National Archives)

A cannon-armed F4U-4B, 97478, of VMF-214 is seen between missions in Korea. The Blacksheep flew from both carriers and airfields. Note the red trim on both the prop hub and tail cone, all other markings are in White. (USMC via M/Sgt. W.F. Gemeinhardt)

Marine groundcrewmen put the finishing touches on F4U-4, 81779, of VMF-312. Operating close to the front line meant being prepared for combat with rifles close at hand, Korea, October 1951. The cowl panel carried White checks over the glossy Sea Blue basecoat. (USMC via M/Sgt. W.F. Gemeinhardt)

F4U-5N Nightfighter, 123183, of VMF(N)-513 loaded with 500 lb. fire bombs and 265 lb. fragmentation bombs ready to fly to its Korean target from a base in Japan. The Flying Nightmares flew Corsairs throughout the Korean War, November 1950. (USMC)

(Left) VC-4 pilot Ens. L.H. Resek recovering his dash 5N on board Leyte nosed over after hitting the barrier with his wheels. The plane completed the flip but the pilot was not seriously hurt. Some of the White letter markings have been resprayed, but do not match. 3 November 1951. (National Archives)

(Above) Glossy Sea Blue F4U-5, 121800, of VF-23 lands on board *Wright* off the coast of Florida, 3 November 1948. (Cdr. R.E. Bennett, USN Ret.)

A flight of four F4U-5Ns of VC-4 patrol just off the coast of Atlantic City, NJ, 25 September 1953. (National Archives)

A 'winterized' F4U-5NL, 124679, No. 51 of VC-4 nosed-up on landing. Note the Black and White 'barber-pole' paint on the arresting hook, NAS Atlantic City, NJ, c.1953. (via Bob Stuckey)

F4U-5, 121862, No. 6 carries the international Orange fuselage band indicating reserve status. The matte Sea Blue anti-glare panel can be seen very clearly on this machine. 1954. (Eric Luhdahl)

F4U-5P, 122021, of HEDRON-MAG-33 carried a K-17 aerial camera in the fuselage mounted on a rotating frame allowing shots to port, starboard or directly below, MCAS El Toro, CA, September 1950. (Warren Bodie)

F4U-5 of VF-21 lands on board *USS Wright* during arresting gear test conducted off the Florida coast. The tail stripe is White. 3 November 1948. (Cdr. R.E. Bennett, USNR)

This F4U-5N, 124665, has been modified to become the XAU-1 (F4U-6). The cheek intakes were faired over and underwing racks to handle ten rockets or bombs were added. Designed as a close support aircraft it was powered by a P&W R2800-83W engine. Overall glossy Sea Blue, the cowl is segmented with White and Red panels. 18 March 1952. (Chance Vought)

AU-1, 129368, No. 153 tied down on a snow-covered ramp at NRAB Minneapolis, MN. In the folded wing position, the AU-1 had a height of just over 16ft. Note the taped-over shell casing ejection chutes just aft of the rocket rails, January 1956. (Bob Stuckey)

AU-1, 129325, makes an arrested landing at NATC Patuxent River, MD. At the moment of arrest, the landing force of this aircraft is approximately three times its weight, 1949. (USN via Hal Andrews)

A later view of the same aircraft, AU-1, 129325, shows it repainted in Marine Markings and displayed on a ramp at Andrews AFB, MD during an Armed Forces Day show, May 1953. (Gordon S. Williams)

Glossy Sea Blue AU-1, 129386, No. 14 from *Flottille 12F* taxiing forward for launch on board the French carrier *Arromanches*, off the coast of Vietnam, 1956. (via Michael Cristesco)

AU-1 No. 9 of *Flottille 12F* totes six 5in HVAR air-to-ground rockets. The prop hub on this Corsair was trimmed in medium Blue, Telergma, Algeria, 1958. (via Michael Cristesco)

F4U-7, 133710, No. 7 returned to the US by France became a restoration project for the USMC Museum at Quantico. Seen here after completion, in US markings, the F4U-7 was basically an F4U-4, MCAS Quantico, VA, 20 May 1967. (Jim Sullivan)